Our Global Community

Games

Lisa Easterling

Heinemann Library
Chicago, Illinois

Customer Service 888-454-2279
Visit our website at www.heinemannraintree.com

Designed by Joanna Hinton-Malivoire
Photo research by Ruth Smith
Printed and bound in the United States of America, North Mankato, MN

15 14 13
10 9 8 7 6 5

The Library of Congress has cataloged the first edition of this book as follows:
Easterling, Lisa.
  Games / Lisa Easterling.
     p. cm. -- (Our global community)
  Includes bibliographical references and index.
  ISBN-13: 978-1-4034-9403-0 (hc)
  ISBN-13: 978-1-4034-9412-2 (pb)
  1. Games--Juvenile literature. I. Title.
  GV1201.E27 2007
  793--dc22
                        2006034293

Acknowledgements
The publishers would like to thank the following for permission to reproduce photographs: Alamy pp. **8** (Danita Delimont), **9** (Robert Fried), **12** (Huw Jones), **15** (Kevin Foy), **19** (Ingram Publishing); Corbis pp. **4** (David H Wells); **7** (Nik Wheeler), **11** (Tom Stewart), **14** (Annie Griffiths Belt), **17** (Ronnie Kaufman), **17** (Jack Fields), **20, 23** (Nik Wheeler; Jack Fields); Getty Images pp. **5** (Stone), **6** (Reportage), **10** (Imagebank), **13** (Photodisc Green); Jupiter Images p. **16** (Dynamic Graphics).

Cover photograph reproduced with permission of Alamy/Ace Stock Ltd. Back cover photograph reproduced with permission of Getty Images/Photodisc Green.

Every effort has been made to contact copyright holders of any material reproduced in this book. Any omissions will be rectified in subsequent printings if notice is given to the publishers.

The paper used to print this books comes from sustainable resources.

062013
007422RP

Contents

Games Around the World

People play games.

People play games for fun.

Games are different from place to place.

Games have different rules.

Types of Games

People play games alone.

People play games with friends.

People play games with cards.

Go Fish is a card game.

People play games with string.

Cat's Cradle is a string game.

People play games with balls.

Soccer is a ball game.

People play games on boards.

Chess is a board game.

People play games on pavement.

Hopscotch is played on pavement.

People play games everywhere.

What games do you play?

Let's Play Hopscotch

1. Draw a Hopscotch board. (See page 19.)
2. Throw a small stone onto Square 1.
3. Hop over that square.
4. Now throw the small stone onto Square 2. Hop over that square.
5. Do this over all the squares.

Hopscotch Rules

1. You must throw the small stone from behind the starting line.
2. The small stone must land in the correct square.
3. You must hop over the square with the small stone.
4. You cannot step on the Hopscotch lines.
5. You can only put one foot in each box.

Picture Glossary

pavement hard covered ground

rule something that you must follow. Games have rules.

Index

Note to Parents and Teachers

This series expands children's horizons beyond their neighborhoods to show that communities around the world share similar features and rituals of daily life. The text has been chosen with the advice of a literacy expert to ensure that beginners can read the books independently or with moderate support. Stunning photographs visually support the text while engaging students with the material.

You can support children's nonfiction literacy skills by helping students use the table of contents, headings, picture glossary, and index.